CARTER AND RYDER

MY LITTLE BROTHER HAS AUTISM!

TM Spivey

ARPress
ILLUMINATING IDEAS.
EMPOWERING VOICES

ARPress
45 Dan Road Suite 36
Canton MA 02021

Hotline: 1(800) 220-7660
Fax: 1(855) 752-6001

Ordering Information:
Quantity Sales. Special discounts are available on quantity purchases by corporations, associations, and others. For details, contact the publisher at the address above.

Printed in the United States of America.
Library of Congress Control Number
ISBN-13   Paperback   979-8-89389-260-4
                eBook   979-8-89389-261-1
                Hardcover   979-8-89389-262-8

Library of Congress Control Number: 2024907063

Our story by TM Spivey

CARTER AND RYDER:

MY LITTLE BROTHER HAS AUTISM!

All Praise and Honor to My God Jehovah through his son Jesus Christ. Without the help I received from my Creator, I would have never been able to write and share my family's story. One day Jehovah God will eliminate all death and disease, and no child or family would have to deal with the system of autism.

With that I heard a loud voice from the throne say:

Look! The tent of God is with mankind,

and he will reside with them, and they will be
his people. And God himself will be with them.

And he will wipe out every tear from their eyes,

and death will be no more, neither will mourning

nor outcry nor pain be anymore.

The former things have passed away.

–Revelation 21:3–4

To:
Ryder and Carter, Daysha, Brandon, Dorothy (my mom),
and to the rest of my family and friends who have all supported me.
Love to you all!

Hi, my name is Carter and I want to tell you the story about me and my little brother Ryder who is autistic.

When I was a baby, all I know is that I felt like a very special kid. My family would kiss me and give me gifts and big hugs all the time.

I went everywhere with my mom, here and there and everywhere! I was living the kid's life. I went to the circus and saw clowns in little cars and animals. That was the life. I learned many things. I wasn't a lonely kid. I was just the only kid.

One day my mom told me that I would be a big brother, and that made me feel happy. I didn't really know what it was like to be a big brother, but I knew things would be different because she said so.

Mom told me to expect another little person just like me to come and live with us and that I would eventually meet my brother or sister soon. I looked out the window every day, and I would wait for my dad to come home and bring my brother or sister.

Mom told me that I would have to be patient and wait just a little while longer before I could see and meet this kid. By the way, I didn't know its name yet but I knew I was going to meet someone very soon.

My mom's dog, Baby, and I would look out the window all the time. I was getting restless because this was taking longer than I expected. Mom tried her best to keep me busy so I wouldn't think about it, but that didn't work because I still thought about it all the time.

Finally, the day came and Mommy brought the baby home and I became a big brother. It was a boy, and Mom and Dad named him Ryder. I was so happy to see and meet him. I was now a big brother.

I took good care of Ryder as he grew bigger and bigger every day. Finally, he began to talk but it was so funny because I was the only one that could understand him. Nobody can understand him because he was just a little baby.

Ryder was getting bigger every day, and I was excited because he was now big enough to play and wrestle with. I noticed many times that my mom and Grandma Meeme would always ask me to repeat what Ryder was saying because they couldn't understand him. I would ask Ryder to repeat what he said, and because we spoke the same baby language, I understood him just fine. It was like we had a secret code, but to me it was normal. I didn't know any difference.

Ryder would say his words very low or where we just didn't understand him.

He would say, "I wuv vu."

Mommy would say, "Oh, Ryder, I can hardly hear you. Carter, can you please tell me what Ryder said?"

"Mom, he says he loves you again."

Then she would say, "Ah, Ryder, Mommy loves you too, baby."

And we both would laugh.

As time went by, we began understand Ryder a little more. We all got used to the way he spoke.

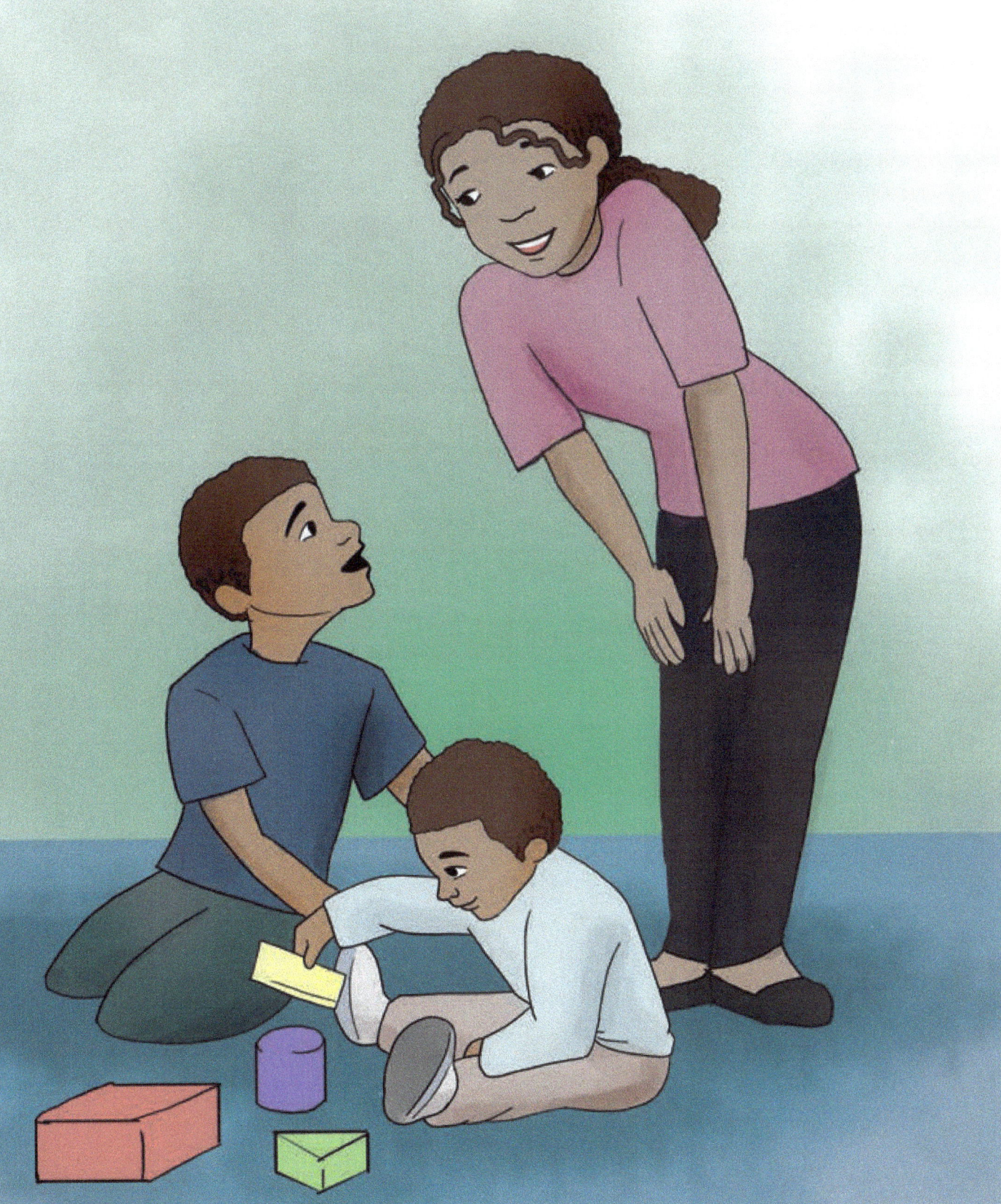

One day I overheard Meeme say to Mom that she was concerned about Ryder because he is still talking like a baby. She asked Mom, "Do you think he could be deaf?"

I didn't know what being deaf meant, but Mom said, "That's a good question, and I have been noticing a few other things about Ryder as well, and I've discussed those things with the doctor. The doctor seems to think he's fine, just a growing boy. He said to just give him more time and he should grow out of it. But if I was still concerned, to just bring him back and he would do further examinations."

Ryder and I always had so much fun together. My parents took us to Lego Land because Ryder loves Legos and camping trips. One time, after one of our camping trips, something happened and my dad was very sad and told Mom it was time to take Ryder back to the doctor for a checkup. I didn't know what it was, but it made me sad too.

I went to school on the day of Ryder's first appointment, and I remember it well because it was the first time I heard the office call me over the school intercom speaker, saying, "Ms. James, can you please send Carter to the office. He is leaving for today!"

All the kids were looking at me and saying, "Wow, Carter, you get to go home early."

I like school, and I have very good grades, but I love getting out of school early too.

We were off to the doctor, and after a few exams, the doctor told Mom, "Let's also get his ears tested, and then we'll know what to do next."

Finally, Mom heard from the doctor, and she told Meeme that it looked like Ryder has some hearing loss and needed speech therapy. Ryder would call me Car-ya instead of Carter. He had a hard time saying his *Ts* and *Ls* and a few other letters. It started getting so bad, I almost couldn't understand him at all.

When Meeme would come to visit, Ryder would say, "Meeme, can me and Car-ya go wit you?"

Meeme would say, "Yes, baby, of course. But you have to ask your mommy if it's okay."

Ryder would not leave me because we did everything together. Where he went, I went too!

Ryder started speech therapy, and Mom thought it would be a good idea to have him tested again because his speech was not getting better but worse. She said that something just wasn't right.

Mom told the doctor that Ryder was acting different. She said to the doctor, "He is complaining of headaches now and says his brain hurts, and he would just start spinning in the floor and waving his hands in the air all the time. He would also cover his ears and cry because he said the noise was too loud. So I bought headphones for his ears."

Those were some of the things she told the doctor. Mommy was really worried now.

The day finally came. All the tests were back, but we took Ryder back in for another exam. This time the doctor said that Ryder was diagnosed as autistic. Mom was a little sad but not surprised because she said she suspected it. She had done a lot of research on autism. It didn't matter because we loved him more than ever. She just wanted to get him the help he needed to have a great life as a person. I really love my brother Ryder. I didn't know what was going on, but I took care of him like a big brother should. Nothing has changed for me either. He was still my pal, and we played and still did everything together.

The big day came for Ryder to start school, and I was officially a big brother bodyguard. While Ryder was in school, he had a very hard time getting along with the kids. He would cry all the time, so Mom would have to pick him up for behavioral problems. She tried to get him in other schools for kids with autism, but some of the schools were very expensive or didn't have any more room for him. Mommy was very sad. I could see it on her face.

In the meantime Ryder continued to go to school and would have to leave early to go to his doctor's appointments, speech therapy, or just not feeling well. When he left school early, I have to leave school early too because Ryder's test would sometimes take a while and Mom would run late picking me up. Sometimes Meeme or my dad would leave early from work and pick me up. I loved going to the doctor with Ryder, so Mom finally decided it was just better to check me out of school when she knew she would really be late, and boy, was I happy!

I would get that call on the school intercom that said, "Ms. James, please send Carter to the office. He is leaving for today!" On the days I left early, my teacher would give me my homework because she knew the challenges with Ryder so my teacher would make sure I had my homework just in case.

Picking up Ryder from school started happening a lot more often, and Mommy said that it was very overwhelming for her and hard for me too. So my parents decided that it was best for Ryder, me, and my family that we were homeschooled.

Well, Ryder's speech has gotten a little better. He has learned many new words. Most of them still do not come out right, but that's okay because he is doing much better around people. We all understand him much better, but now he wears his noise-protection headphones more because he says the noise around him hurts his ears and makes his head hurt, so Mom had to find something to protect his hearing from the loud noise around him.

Mom and Dad got us a new dog named Meech, and I think Meech helps Ryder a lot because he is our protector. Meech thinks he's the big brother now. Meech is such a good dog because he loved playing with us. He would drag Ryder down the hallway by his pants' leg, and we would laugh so hard. We couldn't tell Meech to stop. It was just so funny! Meech is one of the best dogs in the world. He is perfect for me and Ryder!

This is really the story about my little brother Ryder. When this all happened, Ryder was four years old and I was five, just a kid myself. Mommy later told us that me and Ryder would be big brothers, and I was so happy because I knew what that meant right away, but I wonder if Ryder would be as good of big brother as I am one day. My brother is special to my family, and we didn't know he would be a little different in what he does, but it doesn't make any difference. We all love him, and that's what matters!